The awaken st

within you

TEACHINGS OF JESUS IN A DIFFERENT PERSPECTIVE (EMBODY LOVE AND POWER LIKE JESUS)

MM. Mchunu

i

ACTS OF JOHN

"I am a beacon of light to those who see me, I am a mirror to those who look for me, I am a door to those who knock on me, I am a way for you traveller".

Dedicated to you

May this awaken the God in you, allow the Christ in you to awaken and shine the light in you that will enlighten you. Enlighten the whole world and live a world where you are an embodiment of the most high God.

That is my intention for you and the world. When we use the words of Jesus and the bible to enrich our life's, evolve spirituality and transform, when we transform ourselves the whole world will transform.

There is more to us than these physical bodies and these minds, we are a piece of God and we are a particle of the divine and that divinity that is a light within us must be celebrated and embraced fully and we must evoke conditions that will allow the potential in us to turn into a possibility and to allow the possibility to be made manifest. That is why this book was written for you.

ACKNOWLEDGEMENTS

When I first sat down to write this book, I was filled with love and gratitude for humanity. I wanted a way to communicate the word of God to the masses, and there are people who have helped me in that journey to discovering the God in me, and the God in everyone and everything.

Thank you, thank you, thank you Dr Michael Bernard Beckwith your videos and your books have helped a lot and I never met you, but you contributed a lot to my spiritual evolution and hopefully one day I will meet you in person. Not forgetting your wonderful wife Ricky Bee bee and her uplifting music.

Thank you, thank you thank you to the late Rev Ike, I learnt a lot. I learned I was worthy and I found a way to be happy with myself and see God in me, you are a spiritual father to me and for that I am forever grateful.

Thank you, thank you, and thank you to pastor Craig from celebration spiritual centre. Thank you brother, your knowledge and prayers mean the world to me, and those videos mean everything to me us and please don't stop with your good work.

I know I started with people I have never met, but these people have contributed a lot and I love them to pieces. I have experience spiritual growth because of them and I wanted to express my heartfelt gratitude, there are more people and I couldn't mention them all.

I also want to express gratitude to my life partner, thank you for standing by me through thick and thin, and thank you to my little daughter who is an inspiration for me to continue living.

I want to thank my mother Getrude Mchunu Mweli. I love you more than breathing and I will forever be grateful. Thank you for taking me and my little sisters in and giving us a home, after our biological parents died that saved our lives.

Last but not least, I express my gratitude towards all of humanity, I see me in you and I know we are all a reflection of the most high and a manifestation of God. I'm grateful for this experience and opportunity to participate in this human and spiritual evolution.

I'm grateful to the Christ within me that allowed and is allowing the light within me to shine through. **Thank you, thank you, and thank you**

TABLE OF CONTENTS

1. CHAPTER 1: "YOU ARE THE LIGHT OF THE WORLD"

You-that is you the self you have chosen to become, the individual self when you look in the mirror who is looking back. When Jesus says you, he means that you, that you identify with.

Light-this can be love, knowledge and peace.

Let's establish something first, you are made in the image and likeness of God that means you are part God and part human. We don't know what keeps the spirit and body together, so when the creator created you, everything that the creator is you became. I know we have been told that we are worthless sinners, and I say to you God breathed life into you and that life particle became the light, and until you shine your light you will never be free.

The creator is perfect that makes you perfect, and it's hard to believe this but it's true. The light that is within you is needed by the world no matter who and what you are, no one can live the life you live and be you, you must stop hiding the light and let it shine.

The light is love, knowledge and peace, but before you start saying you love other people or you love Jesus you must first learn to love your own self, your three-dimensional self, and how is? This love expressed by your actions.

You will start taking care of yourself, you will watch what you eat, you will watch what you think and importantly you will watch what you say.

If you are made in the image of God, what does that make you? With love and respect you are everything that God is and God is everything that you are. Together we are going to reveal the God in you and you will awaken the Christ within you.

1

So, the light is love, not love focused on a subject, but pure love that is required for anyone to awaken to the truth and awaken the Christ within them. Do this, look in the mirror and say with a smile on your face "I LOVE MYSELF", say it again till you believe it. When you start loving yourself the light within you grows.

Now let's look at knowledge, and it's not science or maths. It's how well do you know yourself. Do you know who you are, at least on the physical level, what do you like and why? What excites you or what hurts you and why? For instance, I love the bible, because I see the bible as a book that describes miracles done by people and these miracles can be repeated. And another reason I love the bible is because I was raised in a church environment.

Do you know why you dress the way you dress, do you know why you talk the way you talk and do you know why you think the way you think. The Christ within you want to awaken, but before you learn about the Christ you must know yourself in and out.

Finally, another thing you need to know its peace. I know we are all praying for world peace and that is impossible, remember the earth and the world is at peace. All of nature is moving and existing in harmony and cooperation, so what is the problem, you me and the rest of the others are the problem, we are not at peace with ourselves.

The world cannot heal when the people in it are hurting, we need to find harmony within ourselves. The media is making us feel inadequate, small and ugly. There are people who hate their noses, their ears, their skin, their hair and even worse their complexion.

The first war is within and if you lose that war you can never find peace in the world. We are all angry at something or someone, truth is we are angry at ourselves, because what you hate in another person is what you hate about yourself.

We project hate and animosity, because that is what already exist within ourselves. To awaken the Christ within us or to let the light shine, we need to find peace within ourselves, and in the following chapters this will be explored in detail.

The world-is a different place and it is experienced differently. The earth is perfect, but the world is imperfect and that is because the world is what we perceive or what we reflect from our own being.

For example, if you are angry and hateful, your world will be filled with angry and hateful people and events. What we project to the world we receive, we all know darkness is bad and it's unknown. Most of the time we are stuck in bad situations and in unknown places, because that is what we are on the inside.

The world is in your hands and you must let the light within you shine bright enough to illuminate you and guide you to heaven. As Jesus said "you are the light of the world", and now we know he meant every man and woman, individually was the light and this is not a group thing awakening is individual.

And the light he was referring to the love, the love you must have for yourself first and then give it back to the world. Remember you cannot give what you don't have, and you must have love for yourself. It is knowledge to know Christ you must know the self and know yourself deeply.

The light also represents peace, and for the whole world to find peace we must find peace first within ourselves, and once you acquire these qualities the light within you grows.

When God created you, he did not leave you. There is a God particle that keeps you alive, it was planted in you in the beginning and then a light came. That light comes in the form of the Christ, it wants to awaken within you. But before you awaken the Christ and shine the light, you must know who and what you are, then work to heal and better yourself.

Keep yourself pleasant, we try a lot to control and shape our reality. It is sometimes, if not all the time impossible, that is because we try to work with something we don't possess. The outside world is impossible to change, because it's a reflection of your inner world.

As a seeker of truth, lover of self and a lover of God you must first work with yourself. And that is to work with the physical, the mental and the emotional. These are the dimensions that make up your dimensional self and if you can work with these your life will change.

The food you eat is important, without any judgement to those who eat meat. You must be conscious of the food you eat, how is the food prepared, and what did it take to get the food on your plate. It's natural for us humans to want to help and heal.

If you saw someone hungry the first thing within you is feed them, and when you see someone angry you want to help them. We can take their stress and disharmony and carry their pain within us, we feel this and we sometimes take is as our own.

Now if the physical body is a living breathing entity and you put dead flesh inside of it, what happens to it, the body wants to live and when you put dead things it will reject them and it will express them through your mind and emotions and the way you feel.

When an animal is killed the sorrow, the anxiety and the pain it experienced it takes with, remember the body is part of the soul and what happens to the soul. All the anguish and hurt, some of it is transferred to the body even in death those qualities remain there, and you consume it and you integrate those feelings of stress, pain and anxiety into your body.

You are what you eat, and the more you consume unhealthy and dead flesh you are in a sense killing your physical body.

The thoughts you think we have been conditioned to think negative thoughts, and this happens unconsciously and these thoughts are not even in the conscious mind, and you cannot help but think these thoughts. And the environment contributes to the thoughts you think.

If you grew up in a church being told about hell and that you are a sinner, and being told that you might go to hell. The thoughts you think will be in accordance to sin, you might not want to think them but they are burned into your mind, and your thoughts will be centred around hell. You will create hell for yourself and for you to awaken the Christ within you, you must get rid of all these negative thoughts you have about the world, God and yourself.

Life is not easy and sometimes it hurts, and sometimes being alive is a pain and it hurts. We hide the real self and we hide how we feel, and that is poisonous. The heart was created to love. Love is your connection to the most high God and when you open your heart, you allow the God in you to shine.

It all starts with you, and the God in you is your alpha and your omega and when you start this journey you will never be alone, because the Christ in you will protect you and provide for you, and you will be divinely guided no matter who or what you are. This is a journey of the soul and for a seeker of truth it is crucial.

Jesus said "you are the light of the world" and the light is Christ within you, and when you learn to take care of your body and take care of your mind and take care of your emotions and put yourself in a state of love and power, you will be in alignment with the divine. The Christ within you will guide and protect you, and the love you feel will be one with you and you will ascend to a different dimension that is called heaven.

Command you me

Every awakened being speak word of power and words that carry authority, that is because they know and they understand their power, and they have awakened to the miracles that is within them and in this piece of scripture this is the God in me talking.

A lot of people have interpreted this wrong, this is not you saying God command me, this is the God in you saying command me, the infinite power that is within you is that its power, but there is no direction just pure power and you must command that power.

We are more powerful than we have been led to believe, that is because we are made by the substance that is pure power and thus pure God. That substance is love and not just the feeling the love, the substance that holds the whole universe together and create and recreate whatever it seeks to create through love and power and that substance is love was love and always will be love or if you prefer God.

How do you command your power, you do it by minding the thoughts you think and the words you speak, all play a part in the reality you experience and your attitude towards the world also shapes your experience.

Jesus was aware of his power so much so that he felt and saw the God he prayed to as his father, and he knew that when he spoke people received healing and people received enlightenment and that power is in you also.

This power was not only given to Jesus, it was and is in every men and women, and our greatest sin is that we deny it. Jesus embraced and lived a life where he was always in power, and that is because he was one with his source of power.

When people came to Jesus, what healed them.it was not Jesus the man, the God in Jesus allowed the God in those people to awaken and heal the sick and open the eyes of the bible, the power and healing was already within them all Jesus did was activate that power and or healing, We find that people released their power through faith and they went to him with the attitude that if I touch his robe I will be healed, and they were healed, that is because their faith in the God in them in their own power was awakened and they were healed.

As a being of light, love and power you must use belief and when you believe in yourself, you believe in the God and your miracles will be a daily occurrence and the works that Jesus did you shall also be able to do.

In spirit, there is no right and there is wrong, and maybe that is why bad things happen to us. Some of the things that happens feel like a burden and they hurt us, and sometimes we feel like small and powerless humans and we don't want to live.

There are no accidents in spirit, there are no punishments and there is no hate, its only love. Through weakness we find our strengths and what you are going through is necessary for you to find your power, and there is a greater reason and a divine plan at work.

We have to come to a place of surrender and that is we need to stop fighting and stop resisting, but embrace who and what we are and take control of our power and whatever the circumstance we must embrace it, appreciate it, learn from it and let it go.

When we fight someone or fight a situation we are giving it power and feeding it energy and that is why war creates more war and hate creates more hate, and that is why we must arrive to a state of surrender and this is not giving up its to stop feeding the situation and just letting it go.

We are pure God, and you might not see it now but this is what we are and we must come to this realization, and the God force in you will create whatever therefore, we must learn to discipline our thoughts and discipline our words and actions.

Through our thoughts, whether we are aware of it or not we create or recreate our reality. Through those thoughts, words and actions we command the God within us, and the God within does what we think, say or do, does not matter whether it is consciously or unconsciously, the only guarantee is that it will be made manifest whether we want it or not.

It is impossible too always think good thoughts, and you cannot live a life where you are always monitoring your thoughts and words, that is why you must always be in a place of love stop fighting and stop resisting.

Love is God and God is power. When you and the most high God are one, you will automatically be in a place of good thoughts and good speech and right action, and you will embody what Jesus embodied and that is love. You will be an instrument of love, peace and harmony, and from that place whatever you command will resemble peace, love and harmony. That is what you will end up becoming, also and from that place the   Christ within you will be awakened.

2. CHAPTER 2: "WOW UNTO, YOU HAVE TAKEN AWAY THE KEYS OF KNOWLEDGE BECAUSE YOU DO NOT ENTER YOURSELF"

Here Jesus was speaking of society and most importantly to churches. We all know churches are a place of worship, and they also supposed to be a place of reconnecting to that part within you, that is God, it is supposed to be a place where you fall in love with life and fall in love with yourself.

Churches are not at peace, because they are run by people who are not at peace, they are now a place where fear is spread and people are told they will rot in hell and will burn for eternity.

If you go to church you must go because you want to, not because you feel guilty and you are trying to buy yourself a way into heaven. But that is why most of us go to church, not because we want to but because are scared and churches are now a place or an institution of fear.

Churches like doctors will never heal you, they will never make you better and as soon as you are healed you stop going to church, so they give you enough and tell you enough to keep you coming back for more. Fear is the best weapon to use against people, because fear makes people feel guilty and then they are bonded by fear to that church.

Keys of knowledge, that is power and that is something that can change your life and change the world and change your whole world. But knowledge is powerful, and knowledge is knowing that you are, what your father is, and if your father is God, then you are also a God. Once you learn about your divinity and learn that the Christ is within you then you are awake.

So, when they have taken away the keys of knowledge, is them not teaching us about our divinity and our beauty. But instead we are taught about our shortcomings and our mistakes and told how long we will burn in hell for them.

God is never judging and God is never condemning, you are judging and condemning yourself and that is made possible, because the power that brings life is the same power that can take it away.

We are punishing ourselves by the thoughts we think, the words we speak and the actions we take. We need to be taught that we are powerful and that we are divine, then we will stop punishing ourselves and then saying its God.

Enter into yourself - the body is the temple and the body needs to be taken care of, needs to be loved, but when you enter into yourself you go above and beyond your body.

When you enter into yourself you need to find out who are we as human beings. We exist in two states the state of being and the state of becoming.

We are always something or someone and we are always becoming something or someone, so how do you enter yourself, first find out what are you thinking and why you are thinking it.

We all think and we are unaware of our thoughts and we don't care, but our thoughts create our reality and every time you think, and every time you entertain a thought you are creating your reality and till you learn to be quite and watch your thoughts you will not enter into yourself.

The next thing to do is watch your feelings, when you enter into yourself you must incorporate the body you need the body, because everything is housed within the body, so when your body temple is taken care of why would you not want to enter into it.

The body temple communicates with us through feelings, why are we feeling the way we feel. A lot of people are addicted to food and they want to keep eating and never look back, and after a while they feel bad and instead of stopping, they continue.

Why when you feel bad about eating you continue eating, it's because your being is craving something big something that is life changing and that thing that is burning you. That craving is you craving to change the world that is you craving to heal the world.

But because of limiting thoughts, limiting speech and limiting actions you talk yourself out of it. This is because you do not feel worthy of your dream or desire, and the reason you don't feel worthy is because you have not learned about your divinity. The keys of the kingdom which are within you and those keys are you. You are beautiful and you are divine and the Christ is within you giving you power and making you a powerful being.

When you have entered into yourself you know yourself and you understand your thoughts and you monitor your speech, because words are creative and you move when you are inspired.

When you have entered into yourself you don't act because you can, you act because the Christ within you is awaken and when the Christ is awakened within you, you are powerful and you are inspired by that divinity in you to move to action, that will change the world because the world within you is healed and made better because you chose to participate.

11

What are the fruits of an individual who have entered themselves, that individual dwells in righteousness. Righteousness is correct and productive thoughts, it's when the mind is the servant and the mind works for you. This is when your thoughts work for you and are aligned with your purpose and are aligned with the God in you.

Righteousness is not only thought it also correct and productive language, unenlightened people talk without thinking and most of the time they are unaware of the way they speak and they are unaware of the words they use, they just talk, words are creative and when you are awakening you must monitor your words.

You might be a person who talks bad about other people, a person who gossips and talks down to people, that is dangerous because what you say about other people it's what you are, it's not that person it's you and when you project negative words to the screen of life those words come back to you.

Righteousness is also correct and productive action, and remember that we said when you have awakened you move. When you are inspired and you are inspired by the awakened Christ within you and your life is made better.

Action is doing and when you do because you are doing out of inspiration, you serve something better and bigger than yourself. When you take back the keys of the kingdom and you enter into yourself you care about what is going on, you love yourself enough to love the world, and your actions reflect that and not only that when you have fallen in love with yourself you fall in love with humanity itself.

In this chapter, we learned that Jesus was talking against those who take away the key, and the main culprits are churches and not only churches society as well everyone who has not entered into themselves has taken away the keys to the kingdom.

It's time we learn and we cultivate right thinking, right speech and right action and that will bring peace to us and to the world, and when you have awakened you will know only love and love will win because only love exists.

Remember, love only exist when an enlightened you is awakened and you know you are divine and beautiful and powerful and worthy too be here and worthy to become the best version of yourself. When you have entered into a state of being, a state where love reigns supreme, and you are the Christ you pray to and you are the God you worship, you not only feel love or crave it you are now becoming love. We all know God is love and to become God we must become love and that is the highest state of being the awakened state.

We need to take care of ourselves, but most importantly we must take care of other people and to do this you must change the way you see other people, and you must not only look at their physical being but see beyond that.

Human beings are entities of love and power, and the love is the God in them and once you see this you realize that the love is God within you, you cannot hate. The substance that created you is love itself and then you have to recognize the power within every human being and the power within yourself.

Human beings are powerful entities. This makes sense how can they be weak when they embody the God of the universe, and Jesus knew this and he understood this he stood tall and proud. He yielded not because he knew that he was more than the body they were torturing, and he continued to love them regardless. This is because when he looked at them he saw his father looking back at him.

Jesus was love itself, and he was power. Even after all these years we are still writing about him, because we feel connected to him and we feel connected to God, when we feel this and acknowledge this than we are a stone throw away from enlightenment.

We must love humanity, because loving humanity means loving ourselves. We must salute the divinity in each man and woman, because we will know that humans are beings of love and power and that demands respect and admiration.

When people fall in love they look radiant and they feel good, I have seen people on their wedding day and all the time they are beautiful, I have never seen an ugly bride and that is because for a brief moment they are embodying God completely and they look and feel radiant with love and power.

We have to know that God is love, but power moves this love and if we are made in the image and likeness of God then we are also love and power. When we learn to ourselves and love our fellow men as we love ourselves, we have tapped in the inexhaustible supply of infinite love and infinite power.

We must learn to admire our reflection-you, them, us, we are all one and thus we are all God.

You-who are you, are you a collection of cells or are you a physical body. When you learn to celebrate yourself, and accept yourself for who and what you are and you love yourself fully. You fall in love with the God in you and when you fall in love with the God in you, the Christ within you is awakening because love is the key.

Them-everyone you meet or spend your time with, your friends, your colleagues and your family, they all represent something within yourself and those people that we like the least they   have more to teach us.

People are a symbol of love, hate, anger or sadness, when you meet someone you feel something and sometimes there are people you know that just pisses you off. You must find out what is it that makes you hate these people, if you are honest you will know that what you want to change in them is something that must be changed in you.

People cannot help but reflect back to you, what you are feeling, thinking and mostly believing. You might say I love humanity and I love myself, but you believe that human beings are untrustworthy you will always be surrounded by untrustworthy people.

What you don't like on the other person is exactly what you don't like about you, when you have awaken to the God in you, you will love everyone and love will be reflected back to you. By your reflection and that is the people you see and talk to daily, learn from them and love them and once their part in your story is over release them with love and gratitude and leave them to the hands of the divine.

Us-together we make up the world as it is, and what puzzles me is that people think that the world is as it is. Us we all have a part to play, if the world is going to heal we need to heal and if the world is going to radiate love. We the powerful species living in it must radiate love, we are in this together and it all starts with you and me and us together we are what the world is and to change it we must first change.

One-once you see divinity in each person and you love each person, and you give to each person, you know that you are responsible for the world being the way it is. Then you will see us all as one a different expression of the one God, when you exist from this dimension you can no longer cause harm to the world or other people or other species, because everything is reflecting you and it's a reflection of what you are and who and what you are becoming.

Love/God-the last reflection is God-the God reflection and this is completion

When Jesus saw himself, what do you think he saw on the reflection back at him, he did not see a man he did not see a teacher or the messiah when he saw his reflection he saw God and that is why the love of God and the power of God was at his disposal.

Jesus said I and the father are one, when you have awaken to your love and to your power you stop seeing a man or woman looking back at you. When you look into the mirror you see God looking back at you, and that reflection is powerful and it's under grace and it is empowered by the source of everything love.

Beyond the mental attitude and beyond the physical body or the emotions that we feel, there lies a spirit that is one with all things, a spirit that is you here and now a spirit that is connected to the divine. When you get out of your way, you will see this and you will feel this and your life will change and the Jesus you read about and admire will awaken in you, and you will become the Christ that is awakening within yourself and you will fulfil the I was and the law is love and love is all and all is God and God is you.

When you see God within you is awaken, and you look into the mirror you see more than a men or women looking back at you. You see the God almighty looking back at you and that is the reflection you strive for and the reflection that you will see, there is no other way and the journey leads to that awakening and Jesus emulated this.

Even on the cross Jesus did not curse or hate men, and that is no matter what they did to him he saw himself in men and he did not see evil, he saw ignorance and he loved men even with his dying breath and the God within him allowed him to forgive us, love us and pay the ultimate price. All was done out of love and compassion for his reflection, and his reflection was us and that is why he loved us. So, and his supreme reflection was God and that is why even on the cross he embodied love.

3. CHAPTER 3: "BE NOT CONFORMED TO THIS WORLD, BUT BE YOU TRANSFORMED BY THE RENEWING OF YOUR MIND"

You must not be bound by the physical world, here Paul was speaking and what he meant was for anything to occur in your life you must change and you must go through a form of transformation.

First let's ponder how are miracles created, and can you create them to transform is a miracle, because you must go against everything that is familiar to you. You must abandon all that no longer serves you and you must change your world and that must be done by a renewed mind and a transformed heart.

We live in a society that has taught us how to be guilty and how to be ashamed of who and what we are, and this causes a lot of hurt feelings and anger on our part. We are not taught how to love ourselves and embrace our flaws and shortcomings but the first step to transforming yourself and renewing your mind is to forgive yourself.

You are bad and everyone is and Christ does ask that you be perfect, because he is perfect for you. Jesus represent a part of you that has never sinned that has never wronged, but that part of you that has been punished mercilessly by everyone including yourself.

You must first forgive yourself and let go of the pain, it's not easy but the most pain is caused by you. You are the now punishing yourself and you project that pain to society and it causes fear and that fear causes worry and you end up stressed, there is a way and the first step is forgiveness.

Listen to yourself and find out how do you feel about yourself, you will often find pain and hurt in yourself or heart and then if it's possible for you find out how it got there, and then forgive the person you feel is responsible for your hurt and your pain and then forgive yourself for letting that person hurt you.

Its different strokes for different folks, when you are ready to forgive you will find a way to forgive yourself and then you must insert gratitude into your life. Be grateful for everything, start with being grateful for yourself, your beautiful body, your radiant face your intelligent mind and your perfect soul and loving spirit, think about how perfect you are in spirit and how much love you radiate and be grateful for that.

You are beautiful as you read this, stop one second and say to yourself "I LOVE MYSELF" the reason is the self is one with everything, you are referring to the God in your body, the mind and every piece that make up the you are renewing right here and right now.

In the same scripture Paul says "don't be conformed into this world", meaning it doesn't matter what you see when you look around and it doesn't matter who you are or who your parents are or are not, this reality doesn't have to define you.

I grew up being taught the world was a big and bad world, and that people cannot wait to betray you and use you. As a result, I grew filled with fear and running away from people and fearing to love and embrace, those fears were not my own they belonged to my mother and I allowed her fears to define me.

I am loving and trusting person to most people this is naïve and I don't care, I love myself and I love my family, I love the world and every day I fall in love with humanity and whether they are aware of it or not. I sometimes look at people from all walks of life I see God looking back at me and I know these are my brothers and sisters regardless of race, financial position, gender or sexual preference.

The world is for you, and humans are good we are just scared to shine our light, because we conform to this world we allow the media and we allow our families and friends project their fears on us, and we walk around with love and joy not expressing it and not sharing it.

To be human is to be God in a three-dimensional body. To be physically separated, but spiritually connected to everything and to be one with the highest self, but not forgetting the lower self, because you need the lower self to understand the higher self. Just like we need this separation to understand our unity and learn to love and heal one another in a dimension of love and peace.

Be you transformed, by the renewing of your mind-you must change. We covered that now we must go deeper and look at the mind, a lot of us are slaves to the mind and we suffer fears that have been programmed in the mind and the mind runs rampant and no one has ever taught us about our own minds.

The mind is a tool that we use to interpret and understand one another on this planet, but for the mind to work for you, the mind needs to be changed and it needs to be disciplined and taught to serve the master.

We are slaves to the thoughts we think and we suffer, because our thoughts are reflecting suffering and all of society is drowning in negative thoughts and horrible habits, we are all at the mercy of the media.

If you notice that whatever the media reports, it gets worse for instance if the media reports on crime, crime goes up. If the news Show cases racism maybe twice that whole week they will have more cases of racism that is because television and computers and radios when they say something it is programmed in the mind and from then we act unconsciously and we produce the same result.

To be renewed we must choose what we experience, and we can do that by rejecting negativity and the people who own the media know exactly what is going on, because we live in a world run by profit, negative things will keep happening and the media will keep promoting those things.

Start by dwelling on positive thoughts and having positive habits. What that does is it creates positive expectations and as you think more and more positive thoughts, you start to expect positive things and guess what positive things happen in your life.

Why did Jesus create so many miracles, it's because he thought positive thoughts and when he prayed he knew God was listening and he expected results, right there and then he did not wish for something and expect its opposite, we must arrive to a place where we pray out of love and thanksgiving and positive expectation.

We are not the mind, we have a mind just like we are not the body, we have a body. This is the truth for everyone and once we learn to love ourselves all of us the physical, the mental and the spirit, and we find a way to forgive ourselves and be grateful. And we learn the power of positive thinking, then we are on our way to transforming and renewing the mind and we are moving to a place where the Christ presence within us can awaken and transform our world.

The world is constantly moving and nothing rest in nature, and we don't want anything to stop, but we in this physical human suit need to stop once in a while. We need to slow down and allow the Christ presence to move inside us and move us to a place where any action will be executed out of inspiration.

"Be still and know I AM GOD"

In this verse, we are told to be still and know that the "I am" is God and now let's explore this phenomena of being still.

Be still-be quite and relax in simpler terms you need to meditate and find a place where you will be quite and you will not move a place of bliss and harmony where it is you, your mind and your spirit.

I am God- whenever in the bible they mention I am, they are referring to you, yes you the small insignificant sinner is God and you might ask how. The bible says you are made in the image and likeness of God that means whatever God is you are and whatever you are is God.

It might sound like blasphemy to a lot of people, but this is the hidden truth and till you learn to embrace this you will forever be lost.

What happens when you become still –you move from physical activity and you stop the body stops trying and stops pushing and everything slows down, and then now activity occurs in the mind, it's you and your thoughts you find out what kind of thoughts you think and why you think them and now you move to a place of acceptance-you accept yourself and you understand why you think a certain way.

Understanding is loving and now you are ready to love yourself wholeheartedly, and then you're thinking activity slows down and then its stops, and now you are nobody and you are nothing at the same time you are everybody and you are everything.

After this you enter a realisation or an awakening, you awaken to your higher self you now exist in a place of love and harmony. You are love itself and you are one with everything, which means you are one with the creator and at that time you understand that the "I am" is what you call God, and that God is you.

It's not easy and it takes time, but this is what you must awaken to in order to awaken the Christ within you. When you learn that God is not a being who is somewhere in the sky, but that God is a being that exist within you. Only then will you have found Christ.

In this chapter, we learned that the physical world does not have to define us and that we can learn to create a world we want to live in. We also learned that fear is the lower self in order to awaken Christ we must be fearless.

We must love fearlessly and we must give fearlessly, and it does not matter who say what, we must choose a life we want to live and we also learned that change is compulsory, a change of mind we must change the way we think and that will affect the way we feel and we must change our actions and remember to change the way you feel about yourself.

Love yourself and love Christ, the Christ that is within you. Forgive yourself, is to love yourself and appreciating is to love yourself and when you are at a place where you are filled with love, you will love humanity.

Why did Christ die in the cross? For us after the pain and humiliation we caused him, he forgave us why? And the answer is his heart and his whole being was radiating and giving love no matter what we did or say he knew only love.

Love is the highest state of transformation and Jesus not only loved us when he looked at us he saw his father in us, he saw himself in us and when we have learned to love completely unapologetically and unconditionally we will look at humanity and see ourselves, and because love is understanding we will understand that all of this is a different   particle of God just like you and me.

Loving one-self is an art and it's not as easy as talking about it and people have a way of hurting and causing us pain that sometimes is hard to forget or forgive, and then we live a life trying to hide our hearts. We think we are protecting our selves, but the truth is when you live a life where your heart is hidden you are as good as dead.

Life is a journey that is filled with a lot of ups and downs, and in that journey we meet people and those people, we call some of them friends and we call some of them enemies. The truth is they are neither friends nor enemies the reason they exist in our reality is, because they have something to teach us and we must learn from them.

Life is centred around each individual learning and perfecting him or herself to a point where he or she has awakened the Christ within, and that individual is ready to live in heaven and live a life where they exist in the dimension that is beyond space and time. To do this we must realize that we must learn from people as much as possible and after the lesson the person will no longer need to exist in your life.

Open your heart, we live with closed hearts and this causes a lot of pain and hurt, and a lot of people are in agony, because they are living with closed hearts and it hurts. It's not protection, its bondage and when your heart is locked up how can you be free because that heart is your connection to source energy. It's time we learned to love and it starts with loving oneself, when you love oneself your heart starts to open up and your life changes because now you live life with an open heart.

Love your neighbour as you love yourself, when you start to love people that are not physically related to you or are not your family. Your heart is opening and when you live your life with an open heart, you get to experience God as

Jesus said God is love so for you to experience God you have to love and you must love yourself first.

Loving yourself -we only love people as much as we love ourselves and we cannot fake that. A lot of people are filled with hate and no matter what they say if there is someone you hate, that is because you have hate within yourself and you hate another, because they represent a part of you that you are not fond of.

We have been taught that we are not worthy of God's love and if you hear this time and time again you start doubting yourself, because unconsciously we all know that God is a dimension within us when someone says this, we unconsciously start despising ourselves.

When you are not worthy of God's love then you are not worthy of your own love and this cause a lot of problems. If God doesn't love because of what you did or what you are doing and then you don't love yourself, how will you love your family or friends and the rest of humanity. We must wash away this feeling of being unloved by God and learn that it is impossible for God not to love us, as God is love so God can only love, and since we are made in his image and likeness we are also love and we must love God and love ourselves so much so that we radiate and embrace love fully and we become the love we radiate.

Look at Africa, a lot of people in Africa are born with a low sense of worth they don't find themselves worthy of anything. This is something we were taught millions of years ago, when our ancestors were sold and bought and were treated as property it is hard to love yourself when you know this but lack understanding of it. You look down upon yourself and you dislike yourself so much that you believe that God himself hates you.

A low sense of worth can only be overcome through love. What do you believe and not whether you believe in God or not that is irrelevant do you believe in yourself. What do you believe you are worth and ask yourself, what do you believe you are capable of doing, having and becoming, your capabilities are the same capabilities as God when you know that you build faith within yourself.

It doesn't matter how black you are and it doesn't matter how ugly you think you are, the almighty God does not do mistake and in the mind of the divine. You are a perfect idea and your beauty and power need to be celebrated and that is something to be proud of it is something to love and celebrate, the power of God that created you and continue to exist within you as you is calling for you to see it and embrace and when you awaken to this you will be free.

When you look in the mirror what do you see? A lot of people see failures and some see unworthy men and women, and some hate what they see and that is because they are looking at the physical body with eyes of contempt and fear condemnation and judgement.

God judges nobody we judge ourselves and we judge ourselves harshly and then we say its God, we don't love ourselves, we don't even like ourselves and we are our biggest critic and we always find ways to hut ourselves and this is the time we transformed our way of thinking, and we changed how we think about ourselves and what we change what we believe about ourselves.

We must be renewed by the transforming of our minds, and I will add by the transforming of our hearts as well, love as much as you can and give as much as you can and forever treat yourself kindly and deserving because you are a perfect idea in the mind, and heart of the most high God and the most high God is perfect and you are also perfect and you were born out of love to love and become one with God and then you   become one with love. Love yourself.

26

4. CHAPTER 4: "IT IS YOUR FATHERS GOOD PLEASURE TO GIVE YOU THE KINGDOM"

The universe, the creator is your father, and you are a child of the universe. The universe delights in making your wishes come true, the universe loves to see you having what you desire.

In spirit, there is no right and there is no wrong, and we define that for ourselves all I know is everything that is happening in your world is necessary. You might not see that or agree within it, but it's true. So now the universe wants to grant you the kingdom.

The kingdom can be anything to perfect health, wealth or a good friend. By now you know and you understand that you play a role in the things that occur in your life, the father is always waiting to grant you your wish,

What is your wish? A lot of people are miserable, not because they lack anything but because they lack a vision for their lives. Life seems stagnate, know thyself-you must know what you want out of life and you must know what you need.

Without vision the people perish

A lot of people die at the age of twenty-one and get buried at the age of sixty, and that is because we live unsatisfying lives and we live life's that lack passion and lack drive and ambition. We have potential to be everything and we choose to be nothing, the prophecy is the one you choose to give yourself.

A lot of people are living lives without purpose, and that is a dangerous way to live and I tell you that for the Christ within you to awaken you must be immersed in a world of passion and light a world, where you are giving and presenting your highest self and that world starts to take shape when you know why you are here, so decide and create a vision for your own life.

Perish is death, and death does not have to occur in the physical human body for us to recognize is, now death has occurred if you look around and you find nothing excites you, a lot of people are sick and tired of being alive.

The work that people do hate it so much that thinking about dying, sometimes dying seems like the only way out, and that is because that job is not for you so stop doing it. We either live someone else's dream or we live someone's else's nightmare, and parents tell us do this and go to school become a teacher or a police man, and we do that because we want them to be happy with us. Now the question is, are we happy with ourselves?

All of it doesn't matter if you are not happy, even finding Christ doesn't matter if you are not happy. That is why you must happy with yourself and find a place where you are loved and you are loving, and you do the things that make you fall in love with yourself. Then fall in love with your world, when your heart is open and you know why you are here, by then you will be ready to shine your light and live as your highest self or you will perish.

In this chapter, we learned that the universe delights in making you dreams come true, and we also learned that you and the father are one. Also, that for you to find Christ you must find yourself and find a place where you can be you and love that you and that place takes form when you know what you want or else you perish.

The message is, there be wary of your thoughts, the universe is always listening. You might think something or saying something unconsciously and you find your world emulating those thoughts and those words, because whether you know this or not your kingdom is created by the thoughts you think and the words you speak and finally by the actions you take.

I used to see myself as a small insignificant human and I prayed that Jesus would save me and somehow make me worthy of God's love. I prayed over and over and over again, and even went to church hoping one day when I die I will go to heaven. Most Sundays I was told how lucky I was that I was here, because of my attendance God might be merciful and I might escape hell.

I was guilty, truth is I knew nothing about God and I didn't love God. How do you love someone so powerful and wrathful, and someone who is always judging and keeping sore of your rights and wrong. Someday I read these words spoken by Jesus **"it is your father's good pleasure to give you the kingdom"**

I asked myself who lives in a kingdom, the answer was royalty this put a smile upon my face. If Jesus said that God who is now my father wants to give me the kingdom that makes me royalty, it was like a light shining on me and from that day I wanted the truth and searched for it myself, and I have come to the conclusion that God is within you and not only that we are all entities of power.

Entity of power - we are strong, not in the physical sense but spiritually and everything is connected to your power, and that power is never ending because that power is God. They make us feel unworthy and small and this contradicts our power and we feel angry and pissed off.

We are powerful beings, only human beings have the power to create a reality and rearrange that reality to suit us and serve us. Only human beings have the power to create co create with the divine, and that is because the kingdom is within us and the kingdom is power, and within the kingdom is where God dwells.

Our thoughts are powerful, so watch what you focus on, and our feelings are power and that is why we attract what we feel good or bad. Last but not least, our words are power, and we create because of the words we speak. This is because the power that created us never left us, it is still within us and when you awaken to your power you empower people by your love and respect their own power.

Power real power never hurts and power is not selfish-power, is what moves love and when you love you become powerful. I am not talking about the power where you have money or influence, I am talking about power that empowers, protects and provides for all the power of God in men.

Power is joy, peace, harmony and it gives strength to love and allow love to create and recreate reality, and that power is given and it a giver not a taker. It is a healer, and when you have it you want to serve and heal humanity, because it is not human power its God power and any men or women that taps into this power they become a living embodiment of God the best example is Jesus.

Radiate power the three unwritten laws of power.

One is help them anyway, powerful people want to get their hands dirty and help their fellow men, and that is because when you are God powerful you see men as a part of you and thus a part of you and you want to help men, and even if you feel they don't deserve it and they don't appreciate help them anyway.

Some people are just horrible and not because they are evil, but because they are ignorant and they use their power to hurt and harm and they have not awakened to the God power within them. You must help them regardless, because once you awaken to the God power you have more to be responsible for.

The next unwritten law of power is forgiveness. You must forgive them anyway. Holding a grudge is giving away your power and even disliking people this robs you of your power. The first thing is forgiving yourself for any ill thoughts or feelings towards humanity and yourself, and just radiate love and power, but for you to be powerful hold no grudge and forgive them even those that don't deserve your forgiveness.

The third unwritten law of power is love, we said that love is all there is for love is God and God is all there is and for any men and women to tap into love they must tap in to love, and you must love and you must love yourself and when you love yourself completely, it extends beyond yourself and you will care about other people because real love is unselfish and real love is powered by the God force.

Love everyone and everything, even in situations you do not like and you love even situations that are not kind to you. You neutralize them and you claim power, form them and then you can walk above them and that is power. And the people that you feel are not deserving of any kind of love, the people you feel are just horrible, you must love those people and love them as you love yourself, because they are as much God as you are and when you love even the least among you, you are one with God and you are one with power and that power moves love.

It is the father's good pleasure to give you the kingdom, you are royalty and the kingdom is within you and God dwells in that kingdom. You are power, you receive it straight form the most high and to remain powerful. Remember to help them anyway, forgive them anyway and love them anyway and always be in position of power and that is the God power, that moves love itself and by doing this you will claim the kingdom that your father wants to give you.

5. CHAPTER 5: "I WILL GIVE YOU THE KEYS OF THE KINGDOM OF HEAVEN"

I will give you - this where Jesus tells us that he will give us the keys of the kingdom of heaven, and how you may ask we grew up being taught that heaven is a place you get to after you have been good here on earth, heaven is like some sort of reward.

The I is the Christ in you, once you learn to love yourself enough you start to trust yourself and you learn to listen to yourself, you develop an understanding that you and Christ are the same person, and that you are worthy and deserving of a place called heaven.

The keys to heaven - the keys are right thought when you dwell in right thinking and when your mind is thinking positive and constructive thoughts. You experience a life of positivity, and not only that you expect good things and good things keep showing up. Right speech nothing is more important than speech, because speech is thought expressed and thought is the ancestor of every action, and when you speak you are bringing your thoughts into manifestation it is crucial that you guard your tongue and watch what you speak and how you speak it.

It is important that you cultivate right thinking and once you do that you won't have to worry about your speech, and it's all automatic. The bible says that the universe was created by speech, so if God created this earth through speech is it possible that you created your world on a daily basis by the words you speak.

Last but not least, its right action everything that we are is reflected in the thoughts. We think those thoughts are translated into words and those words are then translated into action and we act the way we think and speak.

It is impossible to hide who and what you are, because you're authentic self is carried in your thoughts, words and actions. These three, right thinking, right speech and right action are the keys to the kingdom which is heaven.

The kingdom is a multitude of desire, it's unlike heaven we will get to heaven in a bit, the kingdom is desire what do you desire we all searching for peace, love and joy. Just that we brand it differently, it might be a job what will it give you money, and that money is security which is peace of mind you never want to worry about what or how you will eat.

We all want peace and people are stressed worrying about bills and food, and we say if I get that job or earn a certain salary I will stop worrying, I will be at peace because all my bills will be paid. As Christians, we have been told it is bad to pursue money, because money is the root of all evil. But how can you survive in this world without money.

Money is neither good nor is it bad, money does not define you, is what you do with money that defines you. So, if the pursuit of money gives you peace of mind go get it as long as you hurt nobody it is okay.

We must first receive all our hearts desires and then we realize there must be more to life than papers and coins, and then we will seek awakening and enlightenment. But before, that it's all a lie. Why would you seek God on an empty stomach, that is why I say do what you want to do its part of your journey and you need to do it, because from your wanting and needing external sources for peace you will be forced to finally look within.

We also want love and we grew being told we are not worthy of God's love, what does this do? We doubt ourselves and we search for people to love us and it's impossible for anyone to love you when you do not love yourself.

33

Self-love- is God love, because you can only love God the way you love yourself, and it's okay to love yourself we are so hung up on objects we want love to be focused on something or someone to love. Focus love within loving yourself and God will love you the same way, and that love will be reflected from you to you, because remember you are everything that God is and God is everything that you are.

Joy, we all want joy, but joy from external sources is temporary. Joy from within is eternal and when you are happy and not just happy but happy with who you are and what you are, you can find joy. This starts on the physical no matter what has happened to you, find peace with the way you look, find peace with your hair, skin, complexion. Find peace with it or change it and be happy.

We all must find a way to be happy in our own skin, and once we become happy with who and what we are. We are on our way to heaven.

Heaven is neither here or there, heaven is everywhere and once you love the exterior you, you are now ready to love the interior you and you are ready to look within. Heaven can be said to be a state of mind.

How do you feel now, how do you feel about yourself and how do you feel about your world, and right here, right now you can enter heaven and you never have to leave heaven. On the earlier chapters, we said meditate as the bible says be still and know I am God.

In this chapter, we listened to Jesus and he said I will give you the keys of the kingdom of heaven, and we understood that the "I" is the higher self the Christ consciousness that is within us and we also learned that the keys to the kingdom are right thought, right speech and right action. We also learned that we must pursue whatever we feel we need to pursue in order to find ourselves.

We learned that heaven is a state of mind or a state of being, and when you get quite and listen to yourself, and that can be done in a state of meditation you awaken to the Christ within you and you know the truth and understand that the I am is God not a man in the sky you.

Now, this is for the people not ready for the awakening but need to live a life that is fulfilling and live in a way that will allow them to ascend to the awakening when ready, following are three unwritten laws of a successful life.

Life of inspiration - we are all living a life and we are all inspired by someone or something and this is often fulfilling, and that is because we are inspired. It is either we read a book or we see someone, and then we say I want to be like that and then after a while we forget or slowly our energy falls and then we continue living a life that is not changing.

Imagine someone's life was made better because of you, someone saw you and they immediately felt better, and the reason I want you to know that we are all connected and that now is the time to take responsibility and now you must be the inspiration.

When Jesus said I am the son of God, an immense deal of pressure was put in his shoulders and he had to live up to that, to him that was his ideal and then he lived a life that convinced everyone that truly he was the son of God. He even died for that, now who are you, are you like Jesus the son or daughter of God, are you an expression of the most high, are you a spiritual being in a human body, if you answered yes to any of this

Your time starts now you must now live a life of inspiration. It is your duty to find someone who will look up to you, you must find someone who will be inspired by you, you are God and I say that to you, you must now decide whether you live up to that and live in a way that demonstrate God qualities or you reject it and live below your highest potential.

We all need role models and we need people to look up to, and out of that we need to create our ideal self's the kind of person we want to be, our dream self and when we have an image of the person we want to become we will have a vision for our lives and we will not perish.

Time of praising Jesus and saying how good and miraculous he was its over, it's time we become him, it's time we become the Jesus we read about the Jesus that our religion is based upon and a start is by living a life of inspiration.

The second unwritten law is the law of aspiration - we always look up when we pray, and we like star gazing or sun gazing. People of the past used to pray to the sun and created Gods who were always above us, and before aircrafts there was a believe that heaven was above us.

Why would we look up, that is because God created us in his image and we gave God human qualities? God was always a being, that is stronger and more powerful than us and he usually was up in the sky, when we gave God human qualities we made ourselves appear small and insignificant and unworthy.

We say that God is unconditional and perfect, and then we are imperfect and worthless sinners and when the God who created us is all good and the reason I bring this up is, we missed the person and we confused God.

God was created by us and the reason was that we wanted someone or something to aspire to, we wanted life to mean something and we created a perfect being that we all strive to become.

Now God is used to keep people in fear and guilt and get them to give their time and money or they will not get to heaven and I'm not disputing the church. God is you, you in your prefect self, you when you have learned how beautiful and powerful you are that is you when you are perfect and you know this as the absolute truth.

To live a fulfilling life, you must remember who God is or reconstruct the image of God and learn that God is all loving and all-knowing and that God dwells in you and dwells in everything and everyone, because when you awake to that truth you will be praying to a God that dwells in you, God that is a part of you and you a part of God.

Aspire to become God and the best example try to be like Jesus, Jesus was the closest thing we had to God, try to emulate him, he said God is love, try that try to love, love yourself and love your neighbour and it's impossible to love anyone else when you do not love yourself and then love God and aspire to become God.

The third unwritten law of a successful life is the law of contribution - we are all contributing to this world the way it is and we must not lie to ourselves and act as if someone must clean it and make it better, aware or not aware you and I contributed to this world and now is the time we took responsibility.

When we smile we contribute, because someone is effected by that smile. When we frown we contribute, because someone is effected by that frown and it is your responsibility as an expression of God to contribute to a life and a world you would like to live in.

Ill health, stress, poverty and other ills are created by the collective consciousness, look around you what do you not like and ask yourself what would you like to change, and when you have that thing that would like to change think, how would someone change it and then you must then change it.

It might seem small, but I tell you someone life will be made better. It be something silly like a YouTube video and you might think this is stupid and I have seen thousands of videos that just make me laugh and from that video my spirit is uplifted by sometimes a five-minute video.

We are all here to contribute and make the world a better place, but there is nothing wrong in the world we first must make the people living in the world better people, and when we do that a lot changes and the world can transform and it starts with and me, we are all in this together.

Those were the three unwritten laws of a successful life and I assure you when you live a life that you are an inspiration, and you live in accordance with your ideal self and you are always finding ways to live a life where you aspire and live up to the image of God, that is constructive and necessary for your evolution and you contribute to a better world by transforming yourself to a better person, your life will be filled with peace, joy, harmony and success.

Jesus said that God is love, he was demonstrating that is what we must become in order to be God, love and not love the emotion, love the power that create all of the galaxies and the universe and keep our hearts pumping, we must not feel love we must become love.

A lot of people think that there is love and then hate, love is all because love is God and God is all there are no opposites and there are no sides love is all there is and God is all there is just different cases of God, human, plants animals it's all God and to live in the same dimension as God we must become love itself the substance that created us, love yourself and you'll find God

6. CHAPTER 6: "BEHOLD THE KINGDOM OF HEAVEN IS WITHIN YOU"

We have spoken about heaven and the kingdom and in this passage of scripture. Jesus tells us that the kingdom of heaven or the kingdom of God is within us, this was supposed to make things easier but it added to a lot of confusion and in churches this verse is ignored.

It is important that you love yourself, because when you love yourself you are loving a dimension of heaven and you must accept yourself and fall in love with the physical and mental being that you are and then embrace the spirit you.

All of life is a reflection of what you are on the inside, so when Jesus said the kingdom of heaven is within you, he was teaching us that you are everything and you only need to look within to find heaven, and remember I said that you and God are one and now you know that God is heaven and since God exist and can only exist within you, then heaven is another dimension that exist within you.

How do you find heaven within yourself this is complex and often misunderstood, but it's easy all you need to do is be still.

Life is heaven or it is hell you decide what you want it to be life is a reflection of who you are and who you are being.

Heaven a state of love joy and peace and understanding - you are more than your physical body and physical circumstance, so don't let physicality define you, you are more than your mind so don't let your mind define you, find a way to decide and define your own self and be happy with who and what you are and what you are becoming.

We don't have to be taught that hurting another is bad, you feel the pain you cause to another being, and when you do something wrong you know it's wrong, that is because every being is connected to the source we are all connected to that part of us that is in oneness with all.

Take no thought - we are all influenced daily, and taught how to think and how to feel we are told this is right and this is wrong. The media and society have created what is right and what is wrong but the bible says take no thought.

Do not allow the media to define you, do not allow your church to define you/ You are beautiful and you are divine and there is nothing wrong with you, nothing needs to be fixed with you, accept yourself as a spiritual being that you are and embrace and celebrate your divinity.

What is true for you, is hell and punishment true for you? If it is, that is good for you, we all live on the same earth but we exist on different worlds and some people are not ready to awaken and some people are comfortable asleep and we have no right to awaken them without their consent.

Life is not easy and you will go through some test and that might not feel good, but it is necessary for your spiritual growth and everything that is happening needs to happen, and you created it for a reason so did a lesson in your trying times and find pleasure in your pain.

Life is always good and it is for you and whatever you go through is not here to kill you, it's here to heal you and teach you something so find a lesson, because that situation will not leave you till you have found a lesson in it and used it to transcend your limitations and reach your highest potential.

We all pray to a God concept and that is true, because God created men in his image and likeness and we create God in our own image and likeness, why do a lot of people pray and worship a man God who is jealous and angry.

We worship not God but an image of God we have created a concept of God that we created. A lot of people fear God and they fear his wrath and punishment but that does not reflect God that reflects you, the person praying to that God.

It always puzzled me that after Jesus said the kingdom of heaven is within you, why are people still preaching that heaven is in the sky somewhere, and now I know some people are not ready to love and forgive themselves, and that is because people are taught of a God in the sky not a God within themselves and that creates a lot of misguided individuals and causes a lot of problems to.

If you worship an angry God, a God who cannot forgive, a God who holds grudges that does not reflect God that reflects you, those traits exist within you. If you are not ready to let go of that God concept, at least create a loving and forgiving God concept, and remember that whatever you define God as that is also you because whatever you are God is.

In this chapter, we came to the realisation that heaven is a dimension within us and that to get to heaven you must change your God concept and you must learn to love and forgive yourself.

We also learned that our reality is created by our being or consciousness and it's a reflection of who and what we are and what we are becoming. We also learned that if you are not ready to awaken to the fact that you are divine and that you are beautiful and powerful no one has a right to force you.

The kingdom of heaven is within you, so love yourself and take care of yourself and celebrate who and what you are, because by taking care of the self and loving the self you are taking care of God and loving God and that is touching the dimension which is heaven within you, and you can love God directly the way you can love yourself.

The third dimension is not complicated as we might make it seem, and we like to make it seem like things are happening to us. The truth is the life we live is a reflection of who we are being and it is mostly created by the thoughts we think on a daily basis.

As soon as you think those thoughts are imprinted in your reality and you experience the thoughts you think, because when you think you are in a state and we say I'm angry, sad or fearful. When we think we think thoughts that are in accordance with the way we feel and when the way we feel and the way we think is in alignment reality is created because of those thoughts.

Is the solution not to think? No, the solution is to be aware of the thoughts you think and you must be aware of the thoughts you think, and you must not permit anything that you do not wish to manifest in to your life.

Your mind is supposed to serve and help you live the most fulfilling life, and you must find a way to think and lots of our thoughts are centred around ourselves.

Heaven is within you, this makes you divine and powerful and now when you believe this and you know this to be true, you must think thoughts that are serving you and are enforcing the image you have about yourself.

In the previous chapter we spoke about your ideal self who do you want to be, write this down you must write down everything the way your ideal self walks, talks behave and even think, when you do this you will have an image to work with.

The thoughts you think will start to change and they will be centred around that image you have created about yourself, thoughts must serve you, watch yourself and see how are you thinking about yourself to yourself and you must only permit thoughts that are in alignment with your ideal self.

Thoughts are magnetic and they affect everything and they create or tear down your reality, to know that heaven is within you is the truth that was given to us by Jesus and to think and talk in way that reflects this is our responsibility.

Look around you the people in your life and your life conditions, this reflect the kind of person that you are and this also reflect the kind of person the you are becoming and a lot of this is based on the thoughts you think and the words you speak and the feelings you feel.

Remember that you are a reflection of the most high God and keep in mind that your outer world is a reflection of your inner world.

Now you must stop trying to change people and the circumstances you face, all that push and pulling will do you no good. If you want to create a better world become a better person, do not allow the world to change you, you must live your life in a way that the world bends in your will.

The world will collaborate with you and you will meet people who will want to help you, but remember this is your journey and no one can walk it for you and no one can live this life for you, we all connected but each of us has a different mission and now do not allow your thoughts to distract you.

Take no thought - define life and live life by your own terms, and then like Jesus said the kingdom of heaven is within you, go within and find God within yourself and awaken the Christ in you by choosing your thoughts, and finding a way to make your mind serve you and remember your outer world can be changed from within.

7. CHAPTER 7: "HE THAT BELIEVES IN ME, THE WORKS I DO HE SHALL DO AND CREATE WORKS THAT I DO, BECAUSE I GO INTO THE FATHER"

Do you believe in God – if the answer is yes, then you should be living a life of peace and bliss and if your life is not structured the way you want it maybe. That is because you believe in God but you do not believe in yourself, it is useless to believe in God, but lack believe in the self.

You are a being of power that possess the same qualities that the creator has, and it makes sense that the same creative qualities that God has you also have and when you wake up to this you will have faith in yourself, miracles are a daily occurrence to the one who believes in the most high and also believes in his or her capabilities to create miracles on a daily basis.

You need to assess yourself, are you deserving of God's love? Are you worthy of all Gods goodness? And if you don't feel worthy that means you have not learned to love yourself and you have not accepted yourself. Remember you have a body you are more than your body, you have a brain and you can think, but you are more than your mind and everyone knows this just that we don't know how to express and celebrate this.

We live in a dimension that is filled with negativity and people, and situations that just drain your power away. We struggle every day to survive in a world that seems to be condemning and judging us, we either exist in the past where the pain owns us or we seek to escape it by living in the future, but all of life is happening here and now.

We flock to churches and we pray and cry our eyes out wishing and hoping that God forgives us and accepts and loves us, and the feelings of unworthiness and the feelings of powerlessness makes us regret being alive.

God knows only love, the condemning and the judgements are carried out by us and we hurt ourselves, and we say it is Gods will, that is not true. We live in the past and we live by the hormones of stress and pain, and we say I deserve this God put me here, truth is you put yourself there and you are the one hurting yourself, God will never hurt you, we run to the future and this is where a lot of deluded individuals live and exist.

The future we seek, an escape this is either we smoke, drink or take drugs in order or to escape reality and we engage in wishful thinking. The truth is nothing will ever change till you change yourself, and wishing about a better life does not give you a better life and nothing changes until you learn to love and give yourself the respect and love you deserve and you honour yourself to the fullest.

Greater works he shall do - when you are one with the most high God, then you can do great things and for Jesus miracles were as easy as breathing, and that is because he did not have any thoughts that would repel him and convince him otherwise. He believed in God and he believe that he and God were one and the works that God could do he did. So, you must also be convinced of your own power and you must awaken to your possibilities and know your capabilities, and then you will be able to do miracles wherever you go, you will realize that you are a walking and breathing miracle yourself.

I go to the father - Jesus never claimed to have all the power and that is because to have the power he had he had to go to the father, and that is his source and that is where everything for him began and that it where it all ended. He knew that he came somewhere and that after the death of a physical body, the spirit goes somewhere.

The father is source energy and it's the alpha and omega, it's where it all starts and we have explored that the father and you must be one and the same. So, in order to create miracles, you must not only worship and pray to God you must become God, because God is a part of you as much as you are a part of God.

When Jesus says I go to the father he means that he becomes one with God because as soon as he awakens to the power of God he awakens to the power of himself. We now know that God is within us and not only that we know that God is a part of us, and that is the ultimate knowledge and a big step to awakening, knowing that you and the God you worship are one and the same. All that God can do you can also do, because when God breathed life into you he never left you he exists within yourself, all you have to do is go within and you will find God waiting for you. Then you can love yourself and you can embrace yourself and touch that dimension that is and always have been the great I am and that is God within you shining through you for you as you.

We have learned that you and God are one and the same and that we are also a particle or a piece of the most high God, and why now do we keep emphasizing that you love yourself, that is because the more you love yourself the more you love God and the same praise and faith you give God is reflected in how you treat yourself.

In this chapter, we found out that Jesus got his power from his source and that source is available to every living and breathing human being, and once you tap into that source you become one with the infinite power that created you.

We also learned that the more you love yourself the more you love God, and that God is within you and he never left you, we learned that you are a divine and loved being and that miracles can be a daily occurrence for you when you learn to accept them and accept yourself as a piece of the most high, because you radiate power and that power can make manifest whatever you wish for and desire. Also that you no longer have to live in the past or seek escape by running to the future, you can embrace the now and love the now and change your life now by going to the father and that is going within yourself and becoming the God you worship and pray to.

Through prayer one can accomplish wonderful things and can experience and do the miracles that Jesus did, but a lot of people do not how to pray and they don't teach the right way to pray and so before this chapter is over let's explore prayer.

When you say something you usually in a state whether it's a state of love or a state of fear. We know this by finding how we feel when you do something, how do you feel when you say something how do you feel and when you think how do you feel.

Prayer is no different, what matters is how do you feel when you pray, a lot of people pray when they feel defeated and powerless and they drag themselves to their knees and they cry their hearts out and beg God to help them, even though they are worthless sinners and don't deserve any mercy from God.

What blocks prayer and a lot can be said about this but there are three blocks of prayer. Block is negative thinking and negative words a lot of people treat prayer as a time to say all negative words and covey their doubts and confirm their fears and this time they feel worse.

God in a lot of churches is a being in the sky that is jealous and angry so a lot of people often fear God, and desiring is seen as greed. When they pray they feel guilty and bad and they don't want to ask and they convey and dwell in their negative thoughts and negative words.

Negative thoughts and negative words when you speak them you are not purging them out of your system you are merely reliving them and recreating whatever feeling state. So, when you pray and you feel unworthy you will never receive what you are praying for, that is why Jesus never used negative words in prayer because he knew that negative words would neutralize his good work.

Block 2 - is neediness and begging and first you have to know that you need nothing outside yourself, and you need no one and that you are complete everything that you need to survive is already within you, and stop begging.

God is within you and the power you need to move and create anything is already within you, and when you believe this you would stop trying to get this power outside yourself, because this power is within you and it is you.

When you pray don't be needy and don't beg, because that creates a state of lack and that state of lack works against you in neutralizing your prayer.

Block 3 - negative feelings and wishing bad things for other people, when we pray we must come to God with a pure heart, and that is a heart that is free of hate, anger and sadness a heart that has surrendered to the divine plan.

Before praying, how do you feel about yourself and how do you feel about the thing you are praying for, and do you feel you that you deserve it and are worthy of it and finally what state are you in, it is best to pray when you are in a state of joy, harmony or love those states will connect you with the God in you.

Now we know the three blocks of prayer and we know what to watch out for when praying and now the question is, when I pray who is listening? And we all have this question and how are prayers answered, when are prayers answered, and last but not least how one should pray.

When you pray we often look up in the clouds, and that is because we have been told that God is in the sky or heaven above us and this makes us feel small and we try to reach to the heaven above us to get help.

Jesus said that the heaven of God is within you and when you pray you must look within yourself to get to God, and when you do that you touch a dimension within yourself and Jesus also said that God dwells not in temples made by human hands.

God is not in church and the only temple that is not made by human hands, is you he is in you and your physical self. So, God does not dwell in those temples we see outside ourselves and when you pray with an understanding that God is within yourself and you pray in a state of love and compassion and you look to heaven in you in that moment God will be listening.

God is always listening, because God is within yourself and when you pray God is there in you listening.

How are prayers answered - for a prayer to be answered there must be an alignment of thoughts, words and actions before anything comes to manifestation and when you pray you ask for guidance and ask for divine action.

When the God in you is convinced, and that is pray, it's an act of convincing the divine God in you to assist you manifest your dreams and desires, when a person is convinced of anything the first thing they want to do is act they want to do something when you are convinced you don't fold your hands and wait you act.

When you are convinced you start thinking thoughts that help you in the attainment of that dream or desire, and your thoughts will not go against you they will help you, because you are convinced and you feel worthy and that is prayer it is convincing the God in you and convincing yourself that you are worthy and deserving of what you seek and your thoughts and actions are now in alignment.

The bible says that the earth was created by words and that the earth and creation was a thought in the divine mind, and God had to speak for anything to happen you see God was convinced and not only that God was deserving and sure of what creation was going to be like but he had to speak for the earth to manifest.

When you are convinced that what you are praying for is yours, by divine right even the words you speak aid the creation and the attainment of your desire and that thing you are wanting cannot help but come to you, through you.

8. CHAPTER 8: "THE ANOINTING YOU HAVE RECEIVED, ABIDE BY YOU, YOU NEED NOT ANY MAN TO TEACH YOU"

The anointing that is the presence of God is already within you, and everyone is aware of this some people have been taught to reject this and question it. If you are alive you know that there is something more to you than meets the eye, you feel it in your bones.

People all around the world are sick and tired of living in fear, humanity is sick of the killings. We are tired of war and we are tired of living in fear and that fear is eating away at us. We go to war with other people just because they have a different accent or their skin complexion is darker and we are tired of this.

The world is changing, and we have been taught how to hate and fear one another, at first it was surviving and we made it we survived and now all this fear and hatred must come to an end.

Can fear and hatred come to an end when so much money is made from fear and hatred, and all of people are rich because they profit from fear, hatred and pain. But yes, it can come to an end, when you realize that there is something good within you and you wake up to your divinity you will never hurt again.

We all want love and acceptance, and why we want love and acceptance. We seek this outside ourselves, that is because we have not learned to love and accept ourselves and it makes sense why we do not love ourselves, from birth we have been taught there is something wrong with us and that we will never be good enough for God and that if we don't learn to live a certain way we will burn in hell for eternity.

We fight other people and other countries, because we are at war with our own self and you might think I'm not at war with myself, but if you do not love and honour yourself if you deny your own divinity and you reject your higher self you are at war with yourself and that causes problems.

We cannot end the hate and the fear and the hurt until that fear, hatred and hurt is purged from our own selves. When we love ourselves unconditionally only then can we love another, it's impossible to stop the wars until we wake up to the anointing that we received that Christ consciousness that abide within us and you know this and you feel this and you need no man to teach you this.

We are born with an intuitive knowing that there is something divine within us, and we are born loving and giving to ourselves, that love and giving is the Christ within us showing us that we are more than these bodies and that we are all connected to source. Then we are taught how unworthy we are and that we are all born into original sin, I feel this is used to control us and keep us in line.

We are told if we don't come to church every Sunday and if we don't kneel to a certain type of God, a God who is all love but jealous at the same time, we will be thrown into the fire, and we will burn forever and if you teach people fear and unworthiness and self-hatred. What we see in the world will happen, we will hate one another and we will bomb each other for profit.

Once we learn to love ourselves and learn to honour that part of us that is God we will never hurt another. When you wake up to your God nature you realize that we are all one and you respect the connectivity of all humanity, and you learn to love another because when you see yourself as God you realize everything is God, just a different frequency of God and then you celebrate beauty and power of God in all and you become an instrument of love and peace.

We all have a role to play we need to heal one another and we need to heal the planet, it might seem like an impossible task but start with yourself, love yourself and heal yourself remember you are a piece of God. When you love yourself, you love a piece of God and that creates an effect for an awakening of human kind. And because of one loving human being the world is changed for the better you are an expression of the most high, also because of you a new earth is already awakening in you for you and as you and that new earth we call the divine human being who knows and celebrate his or her own divinity.

When a person is born into the world, a light is given to that person and that light allows a person to be alive and exist in this dimension and the birth of any child is celebrated and it should, every child knows that he or she is divine and children know this.

There is something divine about you, the anointing is within you and people call this spirit, I call it the God in men and this God in you stays with you and never leaves you and through intuition it speaks to you, but society has taught us not to trust this voice within us.

We are taught hate and fear from a young age and we grow up and embrace these fears, and we take them and integrate these fears into our personal lives and characters and some people are defined by fear.

Who are you to you, you need to decide whether you are defined by Christ that abides in you or you are defined by your fears and your hatred. The sad thing is that fear and that hatred is not you it's a pervasion of love and power that is designed to work against you.

Every time you hate someone you, are giving your power away and we all know this try being angry for half a day and you will see how tired you become, and you cannot help but be tired because anger and hate and every negative emotion drain you of your power.

The more you hate the weaker you get and the more you fear the weaker you get. The sad thing is these negative emotions and negative feelings are addictive and if you don't act you might end up killing yourself, because they are consuming and they are a current that works against you always.

Jesus said you are the light of the world, and we are all living life without knowing this and we deny ourselves of our greatest. Know this every time you hate and you give into fear you are denying the Christ in you are rejecting the God in you.

The gifts you have only you can give, and the good you have only you can give. By your thoughts or your actions, you are either embracing your good, shining your light or you are denying your divinity and hiding your light, and you are thus depriving the world of a blessing in the form of yourself and the gifts you can give it and the Christ in you is in a way kept in bondage.

The anointing is within you - we are taught to always look outside ourselves and we are taught that love is just a feeling, and that thoughts are just the mind doing what it does no one ever told us that there is a kind of love.

The love that is above and beyond a feeling, the love that is God. No one ever told us that we are to love and not love our children or partners that there is something divine in loving ourselves, and that when you love yourself you are loving God.

We feel that love has to be something that exist outside of yourself, we feel that you need an object to love and that love must be focused outside ourselves, and that love is just a feeling. Love is all there is and when you love yourself unconditionally you have fulfilled the law and you have awakened the Christ within you.

Think of the Christ in you as a seed that was planted in you by the most high God, and when you came to earth you live your life unaware of this seed and unaware of its power. Whenever you fall in love and you give and you accept and when you are truly rooted in the present this seed grows, and whenever you hate or are sad the seed diminishes, and the reason you are reading this is because that seed which is Christ in you wants to grow and wants to grow to a big tree and you are curious how do I do it.

Love is the answer and only love and love, and when you are in love you are in a state of power and the Christ in you rejoice and you are living as your higher self. As your best possible self when you are in love and love is what that seed in your needs to grow and the only way to maintain it is through love and love alone.

The labels that we give to one another keeps us away from ourselves. In earlier chapters, we discovered that other human beings are a reflection of you, that they represent a part of you that is either power or weakness. People represent a part of you that you hate and the people you dislike represent a part of you that you dislike about yourself.

The labels the black or white, the man or female, and the big or small the educated and the uneducated all are keeping us a part. Whatever keeps you from loving your fellow men that is keeping you from loving yourself.

The self is you and all you see and it's all a reflection think about it if you look in the mirror and you saw your reflection whether you like it or not you cannot accept it and it is up to you to love that reflection when God looks at you what does God see.

We all know that God has no body or gender and that God is personified in each men and women, that everything is a reflection of God and that is why God can never punish mankind, and can never hurt or be angry at us because when God looks at us he sees God.

When you see the anointing in you and you have learned to love yourself and give to yourself, that is your fellow men and you have purged all the thoughts of hate and fear and you have learned to forgive and live your life in a state of power and love. When you look at people you see yourself and this is not hard, because love and power awakens you to your reflection.

When you look at your neighbour and you see yourself a different kind of you regardless of the skin colour and the body, it is still you in a different body and having a different human experience then how can you hate that being, because that is you and from that day you will exist and dwell in love always.

People have been taught how to fear what they don't know, that is because we were trying to survive all along, and that in order to survive we have been taught how to flee and we have been running from ourselves and thus running from God.

In God, we are united and we are one. When we see that we are all divinely connected we will cease all this hatred and pain, that we cause to one another because the hurt and pain may be directed at another but it is coming back at you.

We need to end all wars within ourselves and we need to purify the heart and clear the mind, and keep the body in perfect health. When the mind and the body is in alignment, then we can end all wars within and when men has stopped fighting within himself, men will stop fighting amongst themselves.

Where does this fear come from? It all stems from the original sin and we are taught them. According to the bible, the first two people that ate from the forbidden fruit, we were all dammed and sinners even before we were born.

This original sin keeps us in fear and we feel guilty and that guilt keeps us in bondage. We were all born into original blessing and the reason I say this is how do you know its paradise if you know nothing but that place and experience.

The original sin story says that we were all cursed, but take a different perspective and you will see that because of that we were given the greatest power and that is the power to choose.

You and I have a choice, I often see people preaching sermons of fear and condemnation. People are told that if you don't follow God you will burn in hell, and that is bad because it takes away the power of a person to choose.

Jesus said to people **follow me** - that is all he said, he did not say follow me because you will get to heaven or follow me or you will burn in hell. The choice was left to the person follow me, Jesus understood power and he knew that power empowers, and that if you are in a state of love and power you will not take away power of another or impose on their personal will.

Clear but not threatening, and not begging you had a choice and when you did follow Jesus it was out of love and not out of fear, you followed Jesus because you wanted to and he awoke in you love and you saw Jesus as the ideal self.

Today we are coerced to go to church and out of fear and guilt people go to church and this must be done out of love not as a way of buying an entrance into heaven.

Jesus said follow me, and that is because he said himself in you and he loved what he saw and no matter what was done to his body. He never abandoned what he stood for and that is God and he saw God he saw God in you, he saw god in all even in his prosecutors he looked at them and he saw God that is why he could never curse them he could only love them.

He wanted the world to find heaven, because he was in heaven even while still here on earth and he allowed the heaven in him and the light in him to shine without fear, and he knew that one day we will know and understand what he stood for.

Heaven is within every men, women and child heaven is a dimension within every person where God already exist, and that dimension is man's inexhaustible supply and through love and the ability to look within heaven blossoms.

When we have learned to look within and enter into ourselves we will find heaven and we will know how to live in a state of love and power, and we will live a life that Jesus lived a life that is above and beyond the mind and above and beyond circumstances.

In this chapter, we have learned that the anointing which is the light that Jesus saw in every one of us. He saw that the anoint abide in us and that if we kept quiet and learned to listen to ourselves and learned to love ourselves, and that includes everyone we can awaken to the anointing and touch heaven.

We all explored that when you follow Jesus it must be out of love and not out of fear, or as way to buy a ticket to heaven. We found out that Jesus never begged or threaten anyone to follow him it was done out of love and respect for him.

Finally, heaven is within men and the anointing abide within men and the light is within men, and the love we give and share with one another is enough to assist us in reaching another realm of loving and giving and reaching the perfect state of being. Where we are not juts loving we are love itself, and that state we will be a true emanation and expression of the most high God that dwells within us now and always.

9. CHAPTER 9: "I AM THE WAY THE TRUTH AND THE LIGHT, NO ONE COMES THROUGH THE FATHER BUT THROUGH ME"

In this scripture, we hear Jesus giving a direct instruction, and like a lot of scripture it has been taken out of context and misinterpreted.

When Jesus says I am, he is referring to you and it is hard to accept this when you grew up being told how small and insignificant you are and you are told how much of a sinner you are and how undeserving of God's love, the I am is you.

The "I am" is a dimension within yourself a part of you that still remembers that you are God and that you are everything and everything is within you. The "I am" is that connective tissue to the God you pray to. So, first you need to realize that Jesus is speaking about you or a dimension of yourself and then he says the way, the truth and the light.

The way, we all want a way and to a lot of people they like it when someone says do this and they do it, not everyone is excited and wants to find out the truth, and this is shocking but some people lack purpose and they pray that they find someone who will tell them what to do with their lives, and find someone who will say this is the way now walk it, why do you think churches have many followers.

The way is methods that you use to get to heaven and meet the father, when you know yourself and you love yourself, it is easier for you to be still and find God and reach out to the I am that is God within you and awaken the Christ consciousness within you, and then you become the great I am.

The truth-when you are being true, we live in a world that is filled with unauthentic people and a lot of people are trying to be somebody. When you awaken to the truth of your divinity and you realize that everything is within you and that everything is reflecting you and to a certain extent. Everything is you, because you are everything that God is and since God is everything than you are everything as well and that is the truth you must awaken to in order to find heaven and meet the father.

The light – it is moving from darkness to light. It is becoming all understanding, and all giving. It is you existing in a place of love and servitude, not only to serve yourself but to the great I am. How does this happen? When you love yourself and you accept yourself and you are awake to your divinity than now you are ready to meet God.

You know and you have accepted the truth that you and God are one and the same entity that you just exist in different frequencies, once you realize that all is God than now you know that you to are God and that makes humanity an extension of God, then you would want to serve humanity. Because from that perspective you are serving an extension of yourself and nothing brings greater joy.

The father is easy, we now have covered and explained the God question and we have found a way to make it clear to you. To some people it will not make a lot of sense, to some it will sound like rubbish, but to the awake you know that the father, the son and the Holy Spirit are all one and when you become one with them than you are ready to ascend to heaven.

According to Jesus heaven is within you - When you know Christ and you love Christ, you love yourself and you are awake to the love you receive and give to your reflection, which is humanity and you want to serve but how do you get to heaven.

In earlier chapters, we learned that heaven is a dimension within you and that you need not to seek heaven, but all you need is to look inward. How do you do that? It is easier than you might think, it involves you being still and knowing that I am is God.

Be still, we live chaotic lives and we are a generation that is afraid of silence, we are uncomfortable when there is silence. Some people sleep with the TV on or the radio on, and that is so bad that we even forget to take time and shut everyone up and just be still and listen to the higher self.

God speaks in silence and if you never keep quite how will you ever hear God or the divine speaking to you. The noise is to much the external noise and the internal noise it all contribute the chaos and then we express that chaos and we build chaotic societies and we raise chaotic children, all because we never took the time to be quiet.

Jesus finishes of the scripture by saying through me, he is in love with humanity in this point and he is in love with himself and in love with God that he sees the connection of man and God, and the truth is that connection was never lost and it will never be lost because the most high is within us and if that is the case then we are always with God.

When you love yourself and you love Jesus and you love everything, because everything is a reflection of you a reflection of the most high. You then come to the realization that the Christ must be awaken within you for you to reach heaven, and only when you see like Jesus sees and you feel like he feels only then will you understand that to get to heaven is to go through Christ a dimension within yourself. So, you can get to heaven another dimension of your higher self.

When you look within you - You find your way and you find God as Jesus taught us that the heaven of the most high God is within you. When you listen to yourself -you listen to your intuition and that hunch or feeling is God in you speaking to you and you best to listen because sometimes your life is dependent on it.

A lot of people fear the darkness, and we are taught fear from an early age and for the most part fear is necessary but fear must not be allowed to immobilize you and control you.

We often say that everything happens for a reason and that is true and if you look at the world without fear and you relinquish fear you will find that the darkness is necessary, nothing is insignificant and everything has its place in nature.

We must learn to dwell in the darkness, because from the darkness comes light. That means that the darkness is not so bad, but that the darkness is necessary for the light to be born. It is hard and it might not make sense, but whatever you go through you need it and stop fighting your situations, and learn to embrace them and learn from them and grow from them.

The reason we suffer is because we are ignorant of the spiritual laws of life and we go against what Jesus taught us, and we deny our own power and divine identity and we suffer, because that suffering is reminding us that we are more than what we think we are.

The end of suffering is near and soon men and women will awaken to their power and they will claim or reclaim the kingdom, but for this happen we all must agree that if God is good and perfect, and that we are also good and perfect, also that the things that Jesus was capable of doing we also can do because we are the same as the God   we pray to.

What if you saw yourself as God, you will be what would you see.

You need a clear mind and a disciplined mind that is filled with helpful and empowering thoughts and you need a healthy body that is filled with good health and nutrition, and you need an open heart that only entertains that which is pure and good and pure love.

The bible also says without vision my people perish, that is why after that healthy body and healthy mind and an open heart you must have intent, you must have a vision for your life and you must decide for yourself where to go, because after awakening to your power you will realize you can be whatever you want to be.

You will awaken to a state where you are everything and nothing at once, a place where you can love everything and everyone, because you will be seeing through the eyes of the spirit and spirit only sees God. When you see everything and everyone and everything as a reflection of yourself, you will only love and no matter who and what you are or choose to be you will be divinely guided by love peace and harmony and Jesus will be your inspiration.

When Jesus is your inspiration you can only preach that which is good and that which is in harmony with the great spiritual law which is what you give is what you get.

Jesus taught us that you reap what you sow and that left us confused not understanding what he meant. When Jesus said those words, he meant that what you give is what you get, and that is the law and Jesus tried to simplify. This is because at that time we were not ready to awaken to the true power and that is we are a reflection of one another, and we are also a reflection of the most high God that resides within us.

The question is, why do you get what you give and the answer is if any person is a piece of you and you are a piece of that person, because you are a piece of God. And that person is a piece of God or a reflection of both you and God, that means when you give you are giving to a piece of you or your reflection and when you take you are taking from a piece of you or your reflection, and in that sense whenever you give you are giving to yourself.

When you give love to others you receive love and when you give peace and joy that is what you receive, and till you change your perspective nothing will change and every action that is not in harmony with this law, that action is in violation of this law and the results will be suffering.

Suffering is caused by violating, this important law and working against it when you learn this law and you uphold it and you are in harmony with it only peace will be with you now and always.

"I am the way, the truth and the light" and the I am that Jesus is talking about is you not him it is you, so the way is within you travelled by you through you and when you learn to look within yourself and you learn to listen to your intuition and be still you will find your way.

This dimension will be mastered when you have mastered yourself, and you know yourself and love yourself completely and when you do. You will know that everything in your world is a part of your being and a reflection of who you are.

Alpha is omega and the end is one with the beginning, and black is white and one is many, and many are one. This is the end of the game of life and this is the last symptom of awakening and the final stage to the evolution of any spiritual being enjoying this human incarnation now as a God particle in a human body having a human experience.

10. WHY THIS BOOK EXISTS

I have often asked myself why this book exist, and I have found seven reasons as to why I wrote this book.

One - To remind you of who you are - We all live in a world where we want to know who we are and we often take things that are not us. We integrate them to our character and we define ourselves as those things for instance. We define ourselves based on the material things that we have or we define ourselves as the careers that we have.

Who are we really and there is no one answer to this and every answer will be based on an opinion, and this is my opinion of who and what we are. I believe that we are what God is and that means we are spirit and we are particles of the divine.

This means that we are more than our physical bodies, we are more than our minds and we are more than our jobs. We are what God is and that is, divine energy.

The only difference between us and God is that we possess physical bodies, and we are much greater than these suits that we use to have a human experience. Everything that God touches is divine that means this existence is also divine and we must learn to see it that way.

These physical bodies are divine and they are special and without them we cease to exist at least in this dimension, and therefore we must learn to love and appreciate this bodies.

The mind is supposed to be a tool that we use, but it ends up being a weapon against us and we all must learn how to impress our minds with right thoughts and positive thoughts and we must also discipline the mind and having it working for us instead of against us because the mind is a powerful tool.

The mind can rearrange and shift reality as we know it, therefore we must learn to work with our minds remember. I believe that we are a manifestation of the most high so how can we create as God creates and how can we change and rearrange our reality it all starts with and within the mind.

Two - I wrote this book to awaken anyone who will read it that we are divine and not only that we are powerful and we can create what so ever we choose, but also that we have the power and we have a responsibility also and that responsibility is to be in harmony with the at least the one spiritual law.

The spiritual law is - You reap what you sow or you get what you give and that is a divine law after you have awakened to your divine power, and you are ready to create and co create with other divine beings just be sure that you are not in violation of this law.

Three - Another reason I wrote this book was to help people see God in a different light. I wish that humanity could see God as Jesus saw God and that is a father who never left us, and a father who is with us always and not only that as a father that is always within us and that is the God I pray to.

I don't see God as a man or woman, but as everything in creation as a being or spirit that manifest itself in all creation, but not absorbed by its creation and this is the God I wanted to bring to the world a father that dwells within all of us.

Four - Another reason I wrote this book was, because I wanted to free people from fear and the only a way to free people from fear is to make them see that all is created by men through men for men even the after that you experience.

The fear that we create is because there are things that need our attention and those things can hurt us or heal us and as for fear. All of fear is necessary think of fear as darkness and that darkness can consume you, what happens after the darkness has consumed you, you find your light and through the darkness you find the light and through fear will you find your courage and you power but first you need to go through you fear and master is.

Fear is necessary, but it must not own us as I said that we are powerful beings and we are so powerful that if we don't master fear we have the power to create more of it and as long as it dwells within us we will keep creating it.

We live in a world that tells us that we are insignificant, that we are small and powerless, but here is the truth we are strong beyond compare and that our power lies dormant. We must claim it and embrace as long as we deny who and what we are and we deny our power nothing will change when we deny that we are beings created by love and power we deny the creator.

Jesus said we are the light of the world and nothing can be truer than that just that we are the ones that deny this and we forget this and we suffer. We keep denying ourselves. who and what we are and we suffer some more and we suffer so much, because we are ignorant and stubborn so much that we will not give in to our own power and embrace our own divinity and live our lives as particles of God and manifestations of the divine creator.

The **fifth** reason is to awaken the Christ within every person and when I speak of power and love this is what I mean.

Power- Is the ability to change and control to a degree the way your life is and it is you knowing that you are not just an observer and that you have an impact and I know a lot of people fear power.

Power is associated with negative things for instance trying to control people and oppressing people and that is not power, because when you become powerful you will not hurt another or oppress. Because the oppressors are in fear that is why they oppress people and what they have is fear and not power.

When I speak of power I speak of power that is God, power to change your thoughts and change the way you see the world and the power to change yourself and the only way to see power and assess if its power.

Power seeks to empower, and that is true power. When you feel powerful how do you feel about the people around you and how do you feel about the world, and if you are in power you will want to empower those around you and elevate them to your level you will not fear that they will take away your power, because you will be in a place where you have divine power and divine power is you and it is personified by you and no one can take away that power because you become that power.

When you are in a place of power you radiate love peace and joy, and that is true power. No one can feel powerful and be scared at the same time that is why Jesus was crucified. He was never scared because he was always in a position of power, and when you are in a position of power you seek to empower and heal and you care about what is happening in the world and you want to contribute positively.

Jesus said that God is love and I believe that is what everything is and we have thoughts and feelings and actions and even people that we give meaning to. We say that I think negative thoughts and I feel bad and those people are bad people or are evil people, but they are not bad or evil, everything is love and that where it all started and that is where it all will end.

The thoughts you think maybe they are bad or cruel, they are nothing more than a pervasion of love and the feelings you feel are nothing more than love in reverse. So, you must find a way to bring your thoughts and feelings to their natural state and that state is love. When you operate from a place of love you are in a place where power can move, you are in a place where you can experience God, and to remind you of that or to teach you that is another reason I wrote or I am writing this book for you.

Sixth reason - Another reason I wanted to give hope, we live in a society that is just negative and harmful and if you entertain the way people think and feel, you allow other people to determine how you feel and how you think especially about yourself you will be very miserable.

We all need hope and the only way to find hope is find an anchor-an anchor, something that will be the pillar of your power, something that gives you strength and I recommend if you are in a place where you don't see that power within you, trust God or a higher power. But find something that will give you hope and I warn don't make it a person.

I love human beings and now I am in a place where I love every human being on earth and I know it sounds crazy, but as much as I love them I would never make them my anchor. People might not live up to your expectations, and people might not love you as much as you love them and there will be a time when you need them and they are not there. So, for those reasons and other reasons don't make people your reason for being alive, because that reason must give you hope.

My hope is that you read this and you awaken the power within you and you awaken the Christ within yourself and have a deeper relationship with yourself and with whatever you choose to call   God.

When you find hope and you find reasons or a reason to keep breathing, then I would feel that I have succeeded in one of my missions. I know and I understand that life is not easy and I pray that one day you will come to a place where you do not want life to be easier, but you want to be stronger and nothing makes one stronger more than hope.

The **seventh** reason - I wrote this book was to fulfil another mission of mine and that is to promote love, and it is that simple I want us as humanity or spiritual being's whatever labels we give ourselves I want us to love as much as possible.

No matter what kind of God you pray to and no matter your believe systems, we all know and feel that when we love we are in the same state as God, and that is the most natural state. I will say it love is good and love makes everyone feel good, and if we spent time promoting love a lot of the ills in society and the world would disappear.

People might agree with me and then say but, love has no profit because we live in a wold that is runned by profit, and I disagree with that love is all there is and people want to love and want to be loved. When we awaken to that we might change our society and the profit would not be that much important.

Love does not always need an object and sometimes we feel that if there is no one to love, then love is not there. But why do you wake up in the morning whether you are aware of this or not, it is because you love being alive.

God is love and love is good and now before we go around giving endless hugs and kisses, we first must love the most important person in this existence and that person is you, love yourself and love yourself without any fear or condition and from then love your fellow men and love your earth and that is the end of any prophecy LOVE.

11. HOW THIS BOOK WILL HELP YOU

Change is upon you, and the reason you are reading this book is because it is time you also changed or maybe you might prefer to grow to a place and become the person you want to be or seek to be.

This book is not meant to entertain you it is meant to change you for the better to make you a better human being and to help you answer some of the questions you might have about life, the bible and your very own being.

There are three aspects of yourself that must be brought into the light and these aspects of you must change completely in order for you to evolve spiritually, mentally and or physically

One - You need to change the way that you define yourself to yourself and after reading this book you must create a new definition of yourself, I have said time and time again that you are what God is and God is what you are then now it is time you constructed a new definition of yourself that will serve you.

Life is good and life is for you and you must change your approach towards life and I have seen a lot of people live lives where they are victims and they dwell in self-sympathy and self-pity and they are consumed by fear of tomorrow.

When you change your self-definition you are free, society will always aim to know who and what you are or who and what you should be and by choosing for yourself the type of person you want to be and defining yourself as that person everything changes.

After reading this book your definition must be different what are you, now we must come to a place where we love ourselves and we are unafraid to show it and say it a place where we recognize the Christ within ourselves and no matter what we did or did not do every person must come to a place where they celebrate their own divinity.

Why is important to change or create or recreate your self-definition that is because when you have a new definition about yourself you change the way you think and you change the way you treat yourself.

Victims are bullies and those people who are victims have a way of hurting themselves they know before anyone knows that they will not be successful and they are their worst critic and they are their worst enemy and that is because those people choose to define themselves as weak and powerless.

You are a being made by love and maintained by love of the most high and you are more powerful than you can ever imagine and the love you feel for yourself now is necessary in your evolution and you must continue to love and respect yourself and define yourself as love, power and God.

When you redefine yourself, what happens you learn to respect yourself and you learn to appreciate yourself and you feel worthy and deserving of everything and anything that you desire and that is the power of self-definition and I hope and pray that at least you learn that from this book and you are assisted in becoming the best version of yourself.

Two-another aspect is changing your self-image and a lot has been said about this and I won't dwell on it, there is a way that people look at us and people have opinions and ideas of who and what we are and all of that is irrelevant the most important aspect is who and what are you based on you.

We all have an image and images are very important and we as individuals must change the way we see ourselves, when you look in the mirror what do you see and after reading this book you must see an expression of the most high God and you must see a being of power and an instrument of love, peace and harmony and you must rejoice in that knowledge and embrace it fully.

The way we see ourselves is important for instance Jesus saw himself as the son of God and he believed that so much that he was willing to die for it and he had an image where he was always with God and he developed a profound relationship with God and that is the image of Jesus, what is your image and what do you see yourself as and who do you see yourself as, when you are in a place of love and power and you see yourself in a positive light everything changes.

When you look in the mirror what do you see and who do you see looking back at you, that is why I stress that you love yourself and develop a relationship with yourself and love God and develop a relationship with God and then from that place of total love you will be able to awaken the Christ within yourself.

Third-we all suffer from a guilt complex and we are all suffering from guilt and I believe that this book will help you in teaching you how to forgive yourself and get rid of all the guilt that you harbour and feel.

Guilt is bad and what is even worse is un-forgiveness and this is crucial to your development you must forgive yourself and release all the guilt. It is not serving you it is hurting you.

Doing bad things is not right and there is no way around it and everything is necessary and that is true but why feel guilty after what you did and after that lesson was learnt you must then forgive yourself, without self-forgiveness there is no way forward and if you do not learn this then all is lost and I hope and believe that you will find a way to forgive yourself and from there on it will be easier to love yourself and thus love the awakened Christ within you now and always.

These are the last words of Jesus I want to leave you with and this is the inspiration behind this book and I hope you enjoyed it and learned a lot from it.

In second revelations of James Jesus says-**open the door to the way that is within you, so that you may be a guide to those wish to follow the way encourage those who are ready to follow the way and receive its blessings.**

The door needs to be opened and that is the door within you and you need to learn to listen to the God in you and God never left you and God cannot leave you and that is because God is a part of you as much as you are a part of God. The door within you must be opened you must awakened to the truth and the truth is heaven is here and now its dimension within yourself and after learning to look within you will find heaven.

Jesus said "I am the way the truth and the light" and the I am is you, that is why here he says open the door that is within you and the way is path a spiritual journey where you evolve and learn to follow yourself or the Christ in you the way is a way of life and a way of being and no one needs to teach you.

After we become enlightened we have a responsibility and we must be a guide to those who want to follow the way as soon as you awaken to your power and you become powerful you seek to empower those around you.

Jesus also said that you are the light of the world and that is because when you awaken to your power, you become the light and when you are enlightened you light the path for others and the power and the light of Christ is awakened within you.

We need to love ourselves and we need to love ourselves unconditionally and when we do, we will live in a state of love and power and we are grateful for what we are and what we are becoming, we are the light and we become the Christ within ourselves and that light not only enlighten us but will enlighten the whole world.

When you know that you are what God is and you have awoken the Christ within us and you follow the way and you understand that the way is within you and the way is you, you love yourself and you appreciate yourself and you embrace yourselves and celebrate your divinity and you are becoming the God that you pray to

There is something in you that wants freedom and wants to transform you and make you whole and assist you in living to your full potential and you will come to a place that you will question the power within you and you will sometimes want to question and doubt the God in you.

And when you get to that state you must be reminded by Jesus that you are more and you are above and beyond this physical body and this dimension and when you understand this you will know that you live in a world of possibilities and a dimension of heaven and that heaven is always within you.

When you live your life according to the way and you embody the way and you embody peace, love and harmony and you wish you good health and love to all humanity because you came to a place where you see that humanity is a reflection of God and since you are also a reflection of God that means humanity is a reflection of you to. From that place only love can be expressed and only love can be embraced and even those who do not understand can be brought to the light.

Follow the Christ in you and when you get lost and you are in a place of fear or you feel the darkness descending upon you recite these words by Jesus and they will remind you of who and what you are and where to look to find the Christ in you.

The traveller and to the seeker of truth this what Jesus has to say to you, *I am the beacon of light to those who look for me*-when you look within you there is a light and that is because that light within you is the Christ and when you see it you will see that light. The light is an embodiment of love and understanding and the higher truth that dwells within you and you will see that light don't stop looking.

I am a mirror to those who look for me-when you love yourself and see the Christ in you, you will see the Christ in all and when you look in the mirror you will see the Christ in you, like Jesus says that when you look for him he is a mirror and that mirror reflects you and reflects the Christ in you so never stop looking until you see the Christ looking back at you when you look in the mirror.

I am a door to those who knock on me-keep knocking don't stop and keep on asking and keep on trying and when you keep on knocking unto yourself the Christ in you will open the door and you will enter heaven and that dimension within you will be awakened within you and you will enter and dwell with the God in you that dwells with you.

I am a way for you traveller-we are all spiritual travellers and when we find ourselves and we transcend limited thoughts and limited ways and limited words and beliefs and we live life from the way, the way within us and we renew and awaken the Christ in us and from that place we will be divinely guided and loved, and we will follow Christ in this spiritual journey as travellers for Christ, in Christ and as Christ.

Printed in Great Britain
by Amazon

47351051R00051